The Simple Air Fryer Cookbook

Learn How to Prepare Easy, Tasty and Healthy Meals with your Air Fryer

Linda Martin

TABLE OF CONTENTS

INTRODUCTION

An Air Fryer is a magic revolutionized kitchen appliance that helps you fry with less or even no oil at all. This kind of product applies Rapid Air technology, which offers a new way on how to fry with less oil. This new invention cooks food through the circulation of superheated air and generates 80% low-fat food. Although the food is fried with less oil, you don't need to worry as the food processed by the Air Fryer still has the same taste as the food that is cooked using the deep-frying method.

This technology uses a superheated element, which radiates heat close to the food and an exhaust fan in its lid to circulate airflow. An Air Fryer ensures that the food processed is cooked completely. The exhaust fan located at the top of the cooking chamber helps the food to get the same heating temperature in every part in short time, resulting to a cooked food of best and healthy quality. Besides, cooking with an Air Fryer is also good for those that are busy and do not have enough time. For example, an Air Fryer only needs half a spoonful of oil and takes 10 minutes to serve a medium bowl of crispy French fries.

In addition to serving healthier food, an Air Fryer also provides some other benefits to you. Since an Air Fryer helps you fry using less oil or without oil at all for some kind of food, it automatically reduces the fat and cholesterol content in food. Surely, no one will refuse to enjoy fried food without worrying about the greasy and fat content. Having fried food with no guilt is really a form of indulging your tongue. Besides having low fat and cholesterol, by consuming oil sparingly, you save some amount of money, which can be used for other needs. An Air Fryer also can reheat your food. Sometimes, when you have fried leftover and you reheat it, it will usually serve reheated greasy food with some addition of unhealthy reuse oil. Surely, the saturated fat in the fried food gets worse because of this process. An Air Fryer helps you reheat your food without being afraid of extra oils that the food may absorb. Fried banana, fish and chips, nuggets, or even fried chicken can be reheated so that they become as warm and crispy as they were before by using an Air

Fryer.

Some people may think that spending some amount of money to buy a fryer is wasteful. I dare to say that they are wrong because actually, an Air Fryer is not only used to fry. It is a sophisticated multi-function appliance since it also helps you to roast chicken, make steak, grill fish, and even bake a cake. With a built-in air filter, an Air Fryer filters the air and saves your kitchen from smoke and grease.

An air Fryer is really a simple innovative method of cooking. Grab it fast and welcome to a clean and healthy kitchen.

Sausage Breakfast Casserole

Preparation Time: 10 minutes

Cooking Time: 20 minutes

Servings: 4

Ingredients:

- 1 pound hash browns
- 1 pound ground breakfast sausage
- 3 bell peppers, diced
- ¼ cup sweet onion, diced
- 4 eggs
- 1 tablespoon olive oil
- Salt and black pepper, to taste

Directions:

1. Preheat the Air fryer to 355 degree F and grease the casserole dish with olive oil.
2. Place the hash browns on the bottom of the casserole dish and top with sausages, bell peppers and onions.

3. Transfer into the Air fryer and cook for about 10 minutes.

4. Crack eggs into the casserole dish and cook for 10 more minutes.

5. Season with salt and black pepper and serve warm.

Nutrition:

Calories: 472, Fat: 25g, Carbohydrates: 47.6g, Sugar: 6.8g, Protein: 15.6g, Sodium: 649mg

Fried Mushroom

Preparation Time: 25 minutes

Servings: 4

- **Ingredients:**
- 7 oz. spinach; torn
- 8 cherry tomatoes; halved
- 4 slices bacon; chopped.
- 4 eggs
- 8 white mushrooms; sliced

- 1 garlic clove; minced

- A drizzle of olive oil

- Salt and black pepper to taste

Directions:

1. In a pan greased with oil and that fits your air fryer, mix all ingredients except for the spinach; stir.

2. Put the pan in your air fryer and cook at 400°F for 15 minutes. Add the spinach, toss and cook for 5 minutes more. Divide between plates and serve

Pancakes

Preparation Time: 30 minutes

Servings: 4

Ingredients:

- 1¾ cups white flour
- 1 cup apple; peeled, cored and chopped.

- 1¼ cups milk

- 1 egg; whisked

- 2 tbsp. sugar

- 2 tsp. baking powder

- 1/4 tsp. vanilla extract

- 2 tsp. cinnamon powder

- Cooking spray

Directions:

1. In a bowl, mix all ingredients: except cooking spray and stir until you obtain a smooth batter

2. Grease your air fryer's pan with the cooking spray and pour in 1/4 of the batter; spread it into the pan.

3. Cover and cook at 360°F for 5 minutes, flipping it halfway

4. Repeat steps 2 and 3 with 1/4 of the batter 3 more times and then serve the pancakes right away.

Creamy Green Beans and Tomatoes

Preparation Time: 10 minutes

Cooking time: 20 minutes

Servings: 4

Ingredients:

- 1 pound green beans, trimmed and halved
- ½ pound cherry tomatoes, halved
- 2 tablespoons olive oil

- 1 teaspoon oregano, dried
- 1 teaspoon basil, dried
- Salt and black pepper to the taste
- 1 cup heavy cream
- ½ tablespoon cilantro, chopped

Directions:

1. In your air fryer's pan, combine the green beans with the tomatoes and the other Ingredients:, toss and cook at 360 degrees F for 20 minutes.
2. Divide the mix between plates and serve.

Nutrition:

Calories 174, fat 5, fiber 7, carbs 11, protein 4

Okra and Green Beans Stew

Preparation Time: 20 minutes

Servings: 4

Ingredients:

- 1 lb. green beans; halved
- 4 garlic cloves; minced
- 1 cup okra
- 3 tbsp. tomato sauce
- 1 tbsp. thyme; chopped.
- Salt and black pepper to taste.

Directions:

1. In a pan that fits your air fryer, mix all the ingredients, toss, introduce the pan in the air fryer and cook at 370°F for 15 minutes
2. Divide the stew into bowls and serve.

Nutrition:

Calories: 183; Fat: 5g; Fiber: 2g; Carbs: 4g; Protein: 8g

Cheese and Bacon Rolls

Preparation Time: 25 minutes

Servings: 3

Ingredients:

- 8 ounces. refrigerated crescent roll dough [usually 1 can]
- 6 ounces. very sharp cheddar cheese; grated
- 1-pound bacon; cooked and chopped

Directions:

1. Unroll the crescent dough and, using a sharp knife, cut it into 1-inch by 1 1/2 - inch pieces.
2. In a medium bowl; combine the cheese and bacon. Spread about 1/4 cup of this mixture on each piece of dough.
3. Briefly preheat your Air Fryer to 330 – degrees Fahrenheit.
4. Place the rolls in the Fryer; either on the Air Fry tray or in the food basket.

5. Bake until golden brown; 6 – 8 minutes, and enjoy!

6. Note: The timing of this recipe can vary from one Fryer to the next; so watch carefully for the browning of the rolls.

Cabbage and Radishes Mix

Preparation Time: 20 minutes

Servings: 4

Ingredients:

- 6 cups green cabbage; shredded
- ½ cup celery leaves; chopped.
- ¼ cup green onions; chopped.
- 6 radishes; sliced

- 3 tbsp. olive oil
- 2 tbsp. balsamic vinegar
- ½ tsp. hot paprika
- 1 tsp. lemon juice

Directions:

1. In your air fryer's pan, combine all the ingredients and toss well.
2. Introduce the pan in the fryer and cook at 380°F for 15 minutes. Divide between plates and serve as a side dish

Nutrition:

Calories: 130; Fat: 4g; Fiber: 3g; Carbs: 4g; Protein: 7g

Parmesan Zucchini Chips

Preparation Time: 20 minutes

Servings: 4

Ingredients:

- 1 oz. pork rinds.
- ½ cup grated Parmesan cheese.
- 2 medium zucchini
- 1 large egg.

Directions:

1. Slice zucchini in ¼-inch-thick slices. Place between two layers of paper towels or a clean kitchen towel for 30 minutes to remove excess moisture

2. Place pork rinds into food processor and pulse until finely ground. Pour into medium bowl and mix with Parmesan

3. Beat egg in a small bowl.

4. Dip zucchini slices in egg and then in pork rind mixture, coating as completely as possible.

Carefully place each slice into the air fryer basket in a single layer, working in batches as necessary.

5. Adjust temperature to 320 Degrees F and set the timer for 10 minutes. Flip chips halfway through the cooking time. Serve warm.

Nutrition:

Calories: 121; Protein: 9.9g; Fiber: 0.6g; Fat: 6.7g; Carbs: 3.8g

Amazing Onion Rings

Preparation Time: 30 minutes

Servings: 8

Ingredients:

- 2 medium-sized yellow onions; cut into rings
- 2 cups white flour
- 1/2 teaspoon baking soda
- 1 teaspoon baking powder
- 1 ½ teaspoons sea salt flakes
- 2 medium-sized eggs
- 1 ½ cups plain milk
- 1 ¼ cups seasoned breadcrumbs
- 1/2 teaspoon green peppercorns; freshly cracked
- 1/2 teaspoon dried dill weed
- 1/4 teaspoon paprika

Directions:

1. Begin by preheating your Air Fryer to 356 - degrees Fahrenheit.

2. Place the onion rings into the bowl with icy cold water and let them stay 15 to 20 minutes.

3. Drain the onion rings and dry them using a kitchen towel.

4. In a shallow bowl; mix the sifted flour together with baking soda, baking powder and sea salt flakes.

5. Then; coat each onion ring with the flour mixture.

6. In another shallow bowl; beat the eggs with milk, add the mixture to the remaining flour mixture and whisk well. Dredge the coated onion rings into this batter.

7. In a third bowl; mix the seasoned breadcrumbs, green peppercorns, dill, and paprika. Roll the onion rings over the breadcrumb mix, covering well. Air-fry them in the cooking basket for 8 to 11 minutes or until thoroughly cooked to golden.

Cheese and Spinach Balls

Preparation Time: 35 minutes

Servings: 3

Ingredients:

- 1 cup corn flour
- 1 cup bread crumbs
- 1 cup spinach [boiled]
- 2 onion [chopped]
- 1 tablespoon red chili flakes
- 1/2 cup mozzarella [grated]
- 1 teaspoon garlic [grated]
- 1 tablespoon salt
- 2 tablespoon olive oil

Directions:

1. Mix all ingredients and form the mixture into small balls. Brush the pan with oil.
2. Air fry at 390 - degrees Fahrenheit for 15 minutes. Serve them with tartar sauce.

Breaded Shrimp with Lemon

Preparation Time: 15 minutes

Cooking Time: 14 minutes

Servings: 3

Ingredients:

- ½ cup plain flour
- 2 egg whites
- 1 cup breadcrumbs
- 1 pound large shrimp, peeled and deveined
- Salt and ground black pepper, as required
- ¼ teaspoon lemon zest
- ¼ teaspoon cayenne pepper
- ¼ teaspoon red pepper flakes, crushed
- 2 tablespoons vegetable oil

Directions:

1. Preheat the Air fryer to 400 degree F and grease an Air fryer basket.
2. Mix flour, salt, and black pepper in a shallow bowl.

3. Whisk the egg whites in a second bowl and mix the breadcrumbs, lime zest and spices in a third bowl.

4. Coat each shrimp with the flour, dip into egg whites and finally, dredge in the breadcrumbs.

5. Drizzle the shrimp evenly with olive oil and arrange half of the coated shrimps into the Air fryer basket.

6. Cook for about 7 minutes and dish out the coated shrimps onto serving plates.

7. Repeat with the remaining mixture and serve hot.

Nutrition:

Calories: 432, Fat: 11.3g, Carbohydrates: 44.8g, Sugar: 2.5g, Protein: 37.7g, Sodium: 526mg

Bacon Wrapped Scallops

Preparation Time: 15 minutes

Cooking Time: 12 minutes

Servings: 4

Ingredients:

- 5 center-cut bacon slices, cut each in 4 pieces
- 20 sea scallops, cleaned and patted very dry
- Olive oil cooking spray
- 1 teaspoon lemon pepper seasoning
- ½ teaspoon paprika
- Salt and ground black pepper, to taste

Directions:

1. Preheat the Air fryer to 400 degree F and grease an Air fryer basket.
2. Wrap each scallop with a piece of bacon and secure each with a toothpick.
3. Season the scallops evenly with lemon pepper seasoning and paprika.

4. Arrange half of the scallops into the Air fryer basket and spray with cooking spray.

5. Season with salt and black pepper and cook for about 6 minutes.

6. Repeat with the remaining half and serve warm.

Nutrition:

Calories: 330, Fat: 16.3g, Carbohydrates: 4.5g, Sugar: 0g, Protein: 38.7g, Sodium: 1118mg

Glazed Calamari

Preparation Time: 20 minutes

Cooking Time: 13 minutes

Servings: 3

Ingredients:

- ½ pound calamari tubes, cut into ¼ inch rings
- 1 cup club soda
- 1 cup flour
- ½ tablespoon red pepper flakes, crushed
- Salt and black pepper, to taste

For Sauce

- ½ cup honey
- 2 tablespoons Sriracha sauce
- ¼ teaspoon red pepper flakes, crushed

Directions:

1. Preheat the Air fryer to 375 degree F and grease an Air fryer basket.
2. Soak the calamari in the club soda in a bowl and keep aside for about 10 minutes.

3. Mix flour, red pepper flakes, salt, and black pepper in another bowl.

4. Drain the club soda from calamari and coat the calamari rings evenly with flour mixture.

5. Arrange calamari rings into the Air fryer basket and cook for about 11 minutes.

6. Meanwhile, mix the honey, Sriracha sauce and red pepper flakes in a bowl.

7. Coat the calamari rings with the honey sauce and cook for 2 more minutes.

8. Dish out the calamari rings onto serving plates and serve hot.

Nutrition:

Calories: 307, Fats: 1.4g, Carbohydrates: 62.1g, Sugar: 35g, Proteins: 12g, Sodium: 131mg

Cod Fillets

Preparation Time: 20 minutes

Servings: 4

Ingredients:

- 4 cod fillets; boneless
- 1 fennel; sliced

- 2 garlic cloves; minced
- 1 red bell pepper; chopped.
- 2 tbsp. olive oil
- 1 tbsp. thyme; chopped.
- ½ tsp. black peppercorns
- 2 tsp. Italian seasoning
- A pinch of salt and black pepper

Directions:

1. Take a bowl and mix the fennel with bell pepper and the other ingredients except the fish fillets and toss.
2. Put this into a pan that fits the air fryer, add the fish on top
3. Introduce the pan in your air fryer and cook at 380°F for 15 minutes. Divide between plates and serve.

Nutrition:

Calories: 241; Fat: 12g; Fiber: 4g; Carbs: 7g; Protein: 11g

Black Sea Bass with Rosemary Vinaigrette

Preparation Time: 17 minutes

Servings: 4

Ingredients:

- 4 black sea bass fillets; boneless and skin scored
- 3 garlic cloves; minced
- 2 tbsp. olive oil
- 1 tbsp. rosemary; chopped.
- 3 tbsp. black olives, pitted and chopped.
- A pinch of salt and black pepper
- Juice of 1 lime

Directions:

1. Take a bowl and mix the oil with the olives and the rest of the ingredients except the fish and whisk well.
2. Place the fish in a pan that fits the air fryer, spread the rosemary vinaigrette all over.

3. Put the pan in the machine and cook at 380°F for 12 minutes, flipping the fish halfway. Divide between plates and serve

Nutrition:

Calories: 220; Fat: 12g; Fiber: 4g; Carbs: 6g; Protein: 10g

Ginger Cod Steaks

Preparation time: 30 minutes

Servings: 2

Ingredients:

- Large cod steaks: 2 slices
- Turmeric powder: .25 tsp.
- Ginger powder: .5 tsp.
- Garlic powder: .5 tsp.
- Salt & pepper: 1 pinch
- Plum sauce: 1 tbsp.
- Ginger slices: as desired
- Kentucky Kernel Seasoned Flour: +Corn flour: 1 part of each

Directions:

1. Dry off the steaks and marinate using the pepper, salt, ginger powder, and turmeric powder for a few minutes.
2. Lightly coat the steaks with the corn flour/Kentucky mix.

3. Set the temperature in the fryer to 356° Fahrenheit for 15 minutes and increase to 400° Fahrenheit for 5 minutes.: Time may vary depending on the size of the cod.

4. Prepare the sauce in a wok. Brown the ginger slices and remove from the heat. Stir in the plum sauce adding water to thin as needed.

5. Serve the steaks with a drizzle of the prepared sauce.

Trout Bites

Preparation Time: 18 minutes

Servings: 4

Ingredients:

- 1 lb. trout fillets; boneless and cut into cubes
- 1 sweet onion; chopped.
- 2 celery stalks; sliced
- 1 garlic clove; crushed
- 1 shallot; sliced
- 1/3 cup sake
- 1/3 cup mirin
- 1/4 cup miso
- 1-inch ginger piece; chopped
- 1 tsp. mustard
- 1 tsp. sugar
- 1 tbsp. rice vinegar

Directions:

1. Add all ingredients to a pan that fits your air fryer and toss
2. Place the pan in the fryer and cook at 370°F for 12 minutes. Divide into bowls and serve.

Chicken with Cacciatore (Chicken Hunter)

Preparation time: 10-20,

Cooking time: 30-45;

Serve: 6

Ingredients:

- 1 kg of chicken pieces
- 1 onion:
- 2 carrots
- 3 celery stalks
- 1 clove garlic
- 1 glass of red wine
- 400 g peeled tomatoes
- 50 g of olives
- Salt, pepper, parsley to taste

Direction:

1. Clean the chicken and place it inside the basket previously greased with the cooking spray.

2. Set the temperature to 180°C and cook the chicken pieces for 15 minutes.

3. Add the celery mince, carrots, onions, garlic, red wine, salt, pepper, and simmer for an additional 5 minutes.

4. Then pour the tomato and olives and finish simmering for additional 20 minutes stirring chicken and sauce.

5. Once cooked, add a handful of chopped parsley, and serve hot with mash or polenta.

Nutrition:

Calories 233, Fat 7g, 10g carbohydrates, Sugars 2.2g, Protein 34.7g, Cholesterol 98.5mg

Chicken with Carrots

Preparation Time: 15 minutes

Cooking Time: 25 minutes

Servings: 2

- **Ingredients:**
- 1 carrot, peeled and thinly sliced
- 2 tablespoons butter
- 2: 4-ounceschicken breast halves
- 1 tablespoon fresh rosemary, chopped
- Salt and black pepper, as required
- 2 tablespoons fresh lemon juice

Directions:

1. Preheat the Air fryer to 375 degree F and grease an Air fryer basket.
2. Place 2 square-shaped parchment papers onto a smooth surface and arrange carrot slices evenly in the center of each parchment paper.

3. Drizzle ½ tablespoon of butter over carrot slices and season with salt and black pepper.

4. Layer with chicken breasts and top with rosemary, lemon juice and remaining butter.

5. Fold the parchment paper on all sides and transfer into the Air fryer.

6. Cook for about 25 minutes and dish out in a serving platter to serve.

Nutrition:

Calories: 339, Fats: 20.3g, Carbohydrates: 4.4g, Sugar: 1.8g, Proteins: 33.4g, Sodium: 2822mg

Chicken with Yogurt and Mustard

Preparation time: 10 - 20,

Cooking time: 15 – 30;

Serve: 6

Ingredients:

- 500 g chicken breast
- 100 g of white yogurt
- 40 g mustard
- 1 shallot
- Salt to taste
- Pepper to taste

Direction:

1. Place the chopped shallot inside the basket previously greased.
2. Brown for 3 minutes at 150°C
3. Add the chicken pieces, salt, pepper and cook for another 15 minutes at 180°C.

4. Then pour the mustard and yogurt and cook for another 5 minutes.

Nutrition:

Calories 287.1, Fat 8.9g, Carbohydrate 4.3 g, Sugars 1.7 g, Protein43.6 g, Cholesterol 99.9 mg

Mushroom Chicken

Preparation time: 10-20,

Cooking time: 15-30;

Serve: 6

Ingredients:

- 500 g chicken breast
- Mushroom 300g
- 100 g of fresh cream
- 1 shallot

Direction:

1. Cut the chicken into pieces and sliced mushrooms. Spray the basket and chopped shallot into the basket. Set the temperature to 150⁰C and lightly brown for 5 minutes.
2. Add the mushrooms and cook for additional 6 minutes.
3. Finally pour the chicken, salt, pepper, and simmer for another 10 minutes.
4. Then add the fresh cream and cook for 5 min. until the sauce has thickened.

Nutrition:

Calories 220, Fat 14g, Carbohydrates 11g, Sugar 4g, Protein 12g, Cholesterol 50mg

Tandoori Chicken

Preparation time: more than 30,

Cooking time: 15 – 30;

Serve: 4

Ingredients:

- 600 g chicken pieces
- 125 g whole yogurt

- 1 tbsp curry

- 3 tsp of spices for roasted meats

Direction:

1. Place all ingredients in a bowl, flame well and let stand for 1 hour in the refrigerator.

2. Place the pieces of meat in the basket and set the temperature to 160°C

3. Cook the meat for 30 minutes, turning it 1-2 times to brown the chicken on both sides.

Nutrition:

Calories 263, Fat 12g, Carbohydrates 6.1g, Sugars 3.7g, Protein 31g, Cholesterol 135mg

Crispy Honey Chicken Wings

Cooking Time: 35 minutes

Servings: 8

Ingredients:

- 16 pieces chicken wings
- 1/4 cup clover honey
- 1/8 cup water; or as needed
- 3/4 cup potato starch
- 1/4 cup butter
- 4 tbsp. garlic; minced
- 1/2 tsp. kosher salt

Directions:

1. Rinse and dry the chicken wings. Place potato starch in a bowl and coat chicken wings. Add wings to the air fryer, then cook at 380°F for 25 minutes, shaking the basket every five minutes

2. Once done, cook again at 400°F for 5-10 minutes. All skin on all wings should be very dry and crisp.

3. Heat a small stainless-steel saucepan on low heat. Melt the butter, then add garlic. Sauté the for 5 minutes. Afterwards, add honey and salt

4. Simmer on low for about 20 minutes, stirring every few minutes so the sauce does not burn. Add a few drops of water after 15 minutes to keep sauce from hardening.

5. Remove chicken wings from air fryer and pour sauce over. Coat and serve.

Garlic Chicken

Preparation Time: 10 minutes

Cooking Time: 32 minutes

Serve: 4

Ingredients:

- 2 lbs chicken drumsticks
- 1 fresh lemon juice
- 9 garlic cloves, sliced
- 4 tbsp butter, melted
- 2 tbsp parsley, chopped
- 2 tbsp olive oil
- Pepper
- Salt

Directions:

1. Preheat the air fryer to 400 F.
2. Add all ingredients into the large mixing bowl and toss well.
3. Transfer chicken wings into the air fryer basket and cook for 32 minutes. Toss halfway through.
4. Serve and enjoy.

Nutrition:

Calories 560, Fat 31 g, Carbohydrates 3 g, Sugar 0.4 g, Protein 63 g, Cholesterol 230 mg

Bacon Wrapped Herb Chicken

Cooking Time: 15 minutes

Servings: 6

Ingredients:

- 1 chicken breast; cut into 6 pieces
- 6 slices of bacon

- 1 tbsp. soft cheese

- 1/2 tsp. parsley; dried.

- 1/2 tsp. paprika

- 1/2 tsp. basil; dried.

- Salt and pepper to taste

Directions:

1. In a bowl, mix basil, parsley, salt, pepper and paprika. Place the bacon slices on a dish and spread them with soft cheese

2. Place the chicken pieces into basil mix and cover with seasoning. Place the chicken pieces on top of bacon slices. Roll up and secure with toothpick.

3. Place into air fryer and cook at 350°F and cook for 15 minutes

Lamb Stew

Preparation Time: 10 minutes

Cooking Time: 35 minutes

Servings: 5-6

Ingredients:

- 2 lbs of diced lamb stew meat
- 1 Large acorn squash
- 4 Medium carrots
- 2 Small yellow onions
- 2 Rosemary Sprigs.
- 1 bay leaf
- 6 sliced or minced cloves of garlic
- 3 Tbsp of broth or water
- ¼ Tbsp of sp salt (Adjust it to taste)

Directions:

1. Start by peeling and seeding, then cubing your acorn squash. You can use a nice trick which is to microwave the squash for 2 minutes.

2. Slice the carrots into quite thick circles.

3. Peel your onions and cut it into halves; then slice it into the shape of half-moons.

4. Now, place all of your ingredients in the Air fryer and set the feature Soup/ Stew button.

5. Lock the lid and set the timer to 35 minutes.

6. When the timer goes off; release the steam and pressure before opening the lid.

7. Serve and enjoy your stew.

Nutrition:

Calories – 332.7 Protein – 28.9 g. Fat – 6.9 g. Carbs – 38.9 g.

Beef, Cucumber and Eggplants

Preparation time: 10 minutes

Cooking time: 20 minutes

Servings: 4

Ingredients:

- 1pound beef stew meat, cut into strips
- 2eggplants, cubed
- 2cucumbers, sliced
- 2garlic cloves, minced
- 1cup heavy cream
- 2tablespoons olive oil
- Salt and black pepper to the taste

Directions:

1. In a baking dish that fits your air fryer, mix the beef with the eggplants and the other ingredients, toss, introduce the pan in the fryer and cook at 400 degrees F for 20 minutes.
2. Divide everything into bowls and serve.

Nutrition:

Calories 283, Fat 11, Fiber 9, Carbs 22, Protein 14

Chinese Style Pork Meatballs

Preparation Time: 15 minutes

Cooking Time: 20 minutes

Servings: 3

Ingredients:

- 1 egg, beaten
- 6-ounce ground pork
- ¼ cup cornstarch
- 1 teaspoon oyster sauce
- ½ tablespoon light soy sauce
- ½ teaspoon sesame oil
- ¼ teaspoon five spice powder
- ½ tablespoon olive oil
- ¼ teaspoon brown sugar

Directions:

1. Preheat the Air fryer to 390 degree F and grease an Air fryer basket.

2. Mix all the ingredients in a bowl except cornstarch and oil until well combined.

3. Shape the mixture into equal-sized balls and place the cornstarch in a shallow dish.

4. Roll the meatballs evenly into cornstarch mixture and arrange in the Air fryer basket.

5. Cook for about 10 minutes and dish out to serve warm.

Nutrition:

Calories: 171, Fat: 6.6g, Carbohydrates: 10.8g, Sugar: 0.7g, Protein: 16.9g, Sodium: 254mg

Pork Chops and Spinach

Preparation Time: 20 minutes

Servings: 4

Ingredients:

- 2 pork chops
- 1/4 cup beef stock
- 3 tbsp. spinach pesto
- 2 cups baby spinach
- Salt and black pepper to taste

Directions:

1. Place the pork chops, salt, pepper and spinach pesto in a bowl; toss well
2. Place the pork chops in the air fryer and cook at 400°F for 4 minutes on each side.
3. Transfer the chops to a pan that fits your air fryer and add the stock and the baby spinach
4. Put the pan in the fryer and cook at 400°F for 7 minutes more. Divide everything between plates and serve.

Pork Spare Ribs

Servings: 6

Preparation Time: 15 minutes

Cooking Time: 20 minutes

Ingredients

- 5-6 garlic cloves, minced
- ½ cup rice vinegar
- 2 tablespoons soy sauce
- Salt and ground black pepper, as required
- 12: 1-inchpork spare ribs
- ½ cup cornstarch
- 2 tablespoons olive oil

Directions:

1. In a large bowl, mix together the garlic, vinegar, soy sauce, salt, and black pepper.
2. Add the ribs and generously coat with mixture.
3. Refrigerate to marinate overnight.
4. In a shallow bowl, place the cornstarch.

5. Coat the ribs evenly with cornstarch and then, drizzle with oil.

6. Set the temperature of air fryer to 390 degrees F. Grease an air fryer basket.

7. Arrange ribs into the prepared air fryer basket in a single layer.

8. Air fry for about 10 minutes per side.

9. Remove from air fryer and transfer the ribs onto serving plates.

10. Serve immediately.

Nutrition:

Calories: 557, Carbohydrate: 11g, Protein: 35g, Fat: 51.3g, Sugar: 0.1g, Sodium: 997mg

Herbed Leg of Lamb

Servings: 5

Preparation Time: 10 minutes

Cooking Time: 75 minutes

Ingredients

- 2 pounds bone-in leg of lamb
- 2 tablespoons olive oil
- Salt and ground black pepper, as required
- 2 fresh rosemary sprigs
- 2 fresh thyme sprigs

Directions:

1. Coat the leg of lamb with oil and sprinkle with salt and black pepper.
2. Wrap the leg of lamb with herb sprigs.
3. Set the temperature of air fryer to 300 degrees F. Grease an air fryer basket.
4. Place leg of lamb into the prepared air fryer basket.

5. Air fry for about 75 minutes.

6. Remove from air fryer and transfer the leg of lamb onto a platter.

7. With a piece of foil, cover the leg of lamb for about 10 minutes before slicing.

8. Cut the leg of lamb into desired size pieces and serve.

Nutrition:

Calories: 534, Carbohydrate: 2.4g, Protein: 69.8g, Fat: 25.8g, Sugar: 0g, Sodium: 190mg

Saltimbocca Roman Veal

Preparation time: 10 minutes,

Cooking time: 15 minutes;

Serve: 4

Ingredients

- 70-80 g See
- 16 slices of raw ham
- 16 sage leaves
- 20 g butter

- Salt to taste

- Pepper to taste

Directions:

1. Place the meat slices on a sheet of parchment paper. Arrange the ham slices on the meat, put the washed sage leaf, roll, and close with a toothpick.

2. Place the butter in the basket at 150°C. Melt the butter for 2 min.

3. Add the meat and simmer for 6 minutes.

Nutrition:

Calories 323, Fat 18g, Carbohydrates 1.7g, Sugars 0.4g, Protein 29g, Cholesterol 124mg

Breadcrumbs Stuffed Mushrooms

Preparation Time: 25 minutes

Servings: 4

Ingredients:

- 16 small button mushrooms, stemmed and gills removed
- 1 garlic clove; crushed
- 1 ½ spelt bread slices
- 1 tbsp. flat-leaf parsley, finely chopped
- 1 ½ tbsp. olive oil
- Salt and ground black pepper; as your liking

Directions:

1. In a food processor, add the bread slices and pulse until fine crumbs form. Transfer the crumbs into a bowl. Add the garlic, parsley, salt and black pepper and stir to combine.
2. Stir in the olive oil. Set the temperature of air fryer to 390°F. Grease an air fryer basket.

3. Stuff each mushroom cap with the breadcrumbs mixture.

4. Arrange mushroom caps into the prepared air fryer basket. Air fry for about 9 to 10 minutes.

5. Remove from air fryer and transfer the mushrooms onto a serving platter.

6. Set aside to cool slightly. Serve warm.

Air fryer Vegetable Soup

Preparation Time: 10 minutes

Cooking Time: 20 minutes

Servings: 5

Ingredients:

- 2 tablespoons extra virgin olive oil
- ½ onion, chopped
- ½ green bell pepper, chopped
- 2 cloves garlic, minced
- 1 1/2 cups green cabbage, chopped
- 1 1/2 cups small cauliflower florets
- 1 cup chopped carrots
- ½ cup green beans, cut into small pieces
- 4 cups low-sodium vegetable broth
- 1 can diced tomatoes, no salt added
- 1 bay leaf
- ½ teaspoon salt
- 4 cups of chopped spinach
- 15 ounce cannellini beans, rinsed

- ¼ cup chopped basil

Directions:

1. Place olive oil in the air fryer and set to saute. Add onions, bell peppers, and garlic, then cook, stirring often until starting to soften, which will take 2-3 minutes.
2. Put in the carrots, cauliflower, cabbage, and green beans and cook for 4-5 minutes, stirring often.
3. Add the broth, tomatoes, bay leaf, and salt. Turn off the heat, lock the lid, and cook on high for 5 minutes.
4. Release the pressure using quick release, open the lid carefully, and remove bay leaf. Stir in the spinach, basil, and beans.
5. Ready to serve. May drizzle more olive oil on top if desired.

Nutrition:

Calories – 192 Protein – 7.3 g. Fat – 6.6 g. Carbs – 26 g.

Greek Vegetable Soup

Preparation Time: 15 minutes

Cooking Time: 40 minutes

Servings: 4

Ingredients:

- 3 tablespoons of olive oil
- 1 onion, chopped
- 1 clove garlic, minced
- 3 cups of cabbage, shredded
- 2 medium carrots, chopped
- 2 celery stocks, chopped
- 2 cups of cooked chickpeas
- 4 cups of vegetable broth
- 15-ounce fire-roasted tomatoes, diced
- salt and pepper to taste

Directions:

1. Put the olive oil in the air fryer and set to medium heat saute.

2. Add the onions and cook until soft. Add garlic and cabbage and cook for another 5 minutes. When the cabbage softens, add the carrots, celery, and chickpeas. Stir everything to combine and cook for 5 minutes longer

3. Add the broth and canned tomatoes, then season with salt and pepper.

4. Press cancel to end saute mode and cover the pot with the lid set to sealing mode.

5. Set to soup mode and adjust the time to 10 minutes.

6. After completion, release the pressure manually and serve immediately.

7. You may garnish the soup with parsley, feta, or anything you like on soup

Nutrition:

Calories – 412.9 Protein – 6.3 g. Fat – 26.1 g. Carbs – 43.2 g.

Japanese Udon Noodle Soup

Preparation Time: 10 minutes

Cooking Time: 27 minutes

Servings: 2

Ingredients:

- 3 oz. Japanese udon noodles, cooked and drained
- ½ cup green bell peppers
- ½ cup celery
- ½ cup mushrooms
- ½ cup bamboo shoots
- 2 garlic cloves, minced
- ½ green chilli, finely chopped
- ½ cup baby carrots
- 1 teaspoon rice vinegar soy sauce
- ½ inch ginger, minced
- 1 green onion white
- 1 teaspoon rice wine vinegar
- 1 teaspoon red chilli sauce

- 1 tablespoon sesame oil
- Bean sprouts and green onions, for garnish
- Salt and pepper, to taste

Directions:

1. Put the oil, ginger, garlic, baby carrots and onions in the Air fryer and select "Sauté".

2. Sauté for 4 minutes and add bamboo shoots, celery, green bell peppers, mushrooms, soy sauce, rice wine vinegar, chilli sauce.

3. Set the Air fryer to "Soup" and cook for 13 minutes at high pressure.

4. Release the pressure naturally and add cooked udon noodles.

5. Season with salt and black pepper and garnish with onion greens and bean sprouts.

Nutrition:

Calories: 179; Total Fat: 3.9g;Carbs: 30g; Sugars: 2.7g; Protein: 3.6g

Air fryer Minestrone Soup

Preparation Time: 10 minutes

Cooking Time: 35 minutes

Servings: 6

Ingredients:

- 2 tablespoons olive oil
- 3 cloves garlic, minced
- 1 onion, diced
- 2 carrots, peeled and diced
- 2 celery stalks, diced
- 1 ½ teaspoons fresh basil
- 1 teaspoon dried oregano
- ½ teaspoon fennel seed
- 6 cups low-sodium chicken broth
- 28 ounce can tomatoes, diced
- 1 can kidney beans, drained and rinsed
- 1 zucchini, chopped
- 1 Parmesan rind
- 1 bay leaf
- 1 bunch kale, chopped and stems removed
- 2 teaspoons red wine vinegar
- kosher salt and freshly ground black pepper
- ⅓ cup Parmesan, grated
- 2 tablespoons fresh parsley leaves, chopped

Directions:

1. Set air fryer to saute, add olive oil, garlic, onion, carrots, and celery. Cook, occasionally stirring, until tender. Stir in basil, oregano, and fennel seeds, for a minute, until fragrant.

2. Pour in the chicken stock, tomatoes, kidney beans, zucchini, parmesan rind, and bay leaf. Select the manual high pressure setting and set for 5 minutes.

3. When completed, press quick release to remove all pressure.

4. Stir in the kale for about 2 minutes, then stir in red wine vinegar and season with salt and pepper to taste. Ready to serve.

Nutrition:

Calories – 227 Protein – 14 g. Fat – 7 g. Carbs – 26 g.

Air fryer Mediterranean Chicken And Quinoa Stew

Preparation Time: 10 minutes

Cooking Time: 20 minutes

Servings: 6

Ingredients:

- 1-¼ pounds of chicken thighs, boneless and skinless
- 4 cups of butternut squash, peeled and chopped
- 4 cups unsalted chicken stock
- 1 cup yellow onion, chopped
- 2 garlic cloves, chopped
- 1 bay leaf
- 1-¼ teaspoons of kosher salt
- 1 teaspoon of dried oregano
- 1 teaspoon of ground fennel seeds
- ½ cup of uncooked quinoa
- 1-ounce of olives, sliced and pitted

Directions:

1. Combine the chicken, squash, stock, onion, garlic, bay leaf, salt, ground fennel seeds, oregano, and pepper in your air fryer. Cover the lid, turn the valve to seal and cook on high pressure for 8 minutes.

2. Release the valve carefully, using mitts or tongs. Quick-release until the steam and pressure go down. Remove chicken, then add quinoa to the air fryer, turn to saute and cook while occasionally stirring until the quinoa is tender.

3. Shred the chicken and stir into stew. Discard bay leaf.

4. Serve the soup up into separate bowls, and sprinkle sliced olives.

Nutrition:

Calories – 243 Protein – 25 g. Fat – 6 g. Carbs – 24 g.

Basil Tomatoes (Vegan)

Servings: 2

Preparation Time: 10 minutes

Cooking Time: 10 minutes

Ingredients

- 2 tomatoes, halved
- Olive oil cooking spray
- Salt and ground black pepper, as required
- 1 tablespoon fresh basil, chopped

Directions:

1. Set the temperature of air fryer to 320 degrees F. Grease an air fryer basket.
2. Spray the tomato halves evenly with cooking spray and sprinkle with salt, black pepper and basil.
3. Arrange tomato halves into the prepared air fryer basket, cut sides up.
4. Air fry for about 10 minutes or until desired doneness.

5. Remove from air fryer and transfer the tomatoes onto serving plates.

6. Serve warm.

Nutrition:

Calories: 22, Carbohydrate: 4.8g, Protein: 1.1g, Fat: 4.8g, Sugar: 3.2g, Sodium: 84mg

Fennel Spread

Preparation Time: 25 minutes

Servings: 8

Ingredients:

- 3 fennel bulbs; trimmed and cut into wedges
- 4 garlic cloves; minced
- ¼ cup parmesan; grated
- 3 tbsp. olive oil

- A pinch of salt and black pepper

Directions:

1. Put the fennel in the air fryer's basket and bake at 380°F for 20 minutes.
2. In a blender, combine the roasted fennel with the rest of the ingredients and pulse well
3. Put the spread in a ramekin, introduce it in the fryer and cook at 380°F for 5 minutes more
4. Divide into bowls and serve as a dip.

Nutrition:

Calories: 240; Fat: 11g; Fiber: 3g; Carbs: 4g; Protein: 12g

Sweet Pepper Poppers

Preparation Time: 23 minutes

Servings: 16 halves

Ingredients:

- 8 mini sweet peppers
- 4 slices sugar-free bacon; cooked and crumbled
- ¼ cup shredded pepper jack cheese
- 4 oz. full-fat cream cheese; softened.

Directions:

1. Remove the tops from the peppers and slice each one in half lengthwise. Use a small knife to remove seeds and membranes

2. In a small bowl, mix cream cheese, bacon and pepper jack

3. Place 3 tsp. of the mixture into each sweet pepper and press down smooth. Place into the fryer basket. Adjust the temperature to 400 Degrees F and set the timer for 8 minutes. Serve warm.

Nutrition:

Calories: 176; Protein: 7.4g; Fiber: 0.9g; Fat: 13.4g; Carbs: 3.6g

Buttered Dinner Rolls

Preparation Time: 15 minutes

Cooking Time: 30 minutes

Servings: 12

Ingredients:

- 1 cup milk
- 3 cups plain flour
- 7½ tablespoons unsalted butter
- 1 tablespoon coconut oil
- 1 tablespoon olive oil
- 1 teaspoon yeast
- Salt and black pepper, to taste

Directions:

1. Preheat the Air fryer to 360 degree F and grease an Air fryer basket.
2. Put olive oil, milk and coconut oil in a pan and cook for about 3 minutes.
3. Remove from the heat and mix well.

4. Mix together plain flour, yeast, butter, salt and black pepper in a large bowl.

5. Knead well for about 5 minutes until a dough is formed.

6. Cover the dough with a damp cloth and keep aside for about 5 minutes in a warm place.

7. Knead the dough for about 5 minutes again with your hands.

8. Cover the dough with a damp cloth and keep aside for about 30 minutes in a warm place.

9. Divide the dough into 12 equal pieces and roll each into a ball.

10. Arrange 6 balls into the Air fryer basket in a single layer and cook for about 15 minutes.

11. Repeat with the remaining balls and serve warm.

Nutrition:

Calories: 208, Fat: 10.3g, Carbohydrates: 25g, Sugar: 1g, Protein: 4.1g, Sodium: 73mg

Bacon Filled Poppers

Preparation Time: 5 minutes

Cooking Time: 15 minutes

Servings: 4

Ingredients:

- 4 strips crispy cooked bacon
- 3 tablespoons butter
- ½ cup jalapeno peppers, diced
- 2/3 cup almond flour
- 2 oz. Cheddar cheese, white, shredded
- 1 pinch cayenne pepper
- 1 tablespoon bacon fat
- 1 teaspoon kosher salt
- Black pepper, ground, to taste

Directions:

1. Preheat the Air fryer to 390 degree F and grease an Air fryer basket.
2. Mix together butter with salt and water on medium heat in a skillet.

3. Whisk in the flour and sauté for about 3 minutes.

4. Dish out in a bowl and mix with the remaining ingredients to form a dough.

5. Wrap plastic wrap around the dough and refrigerate for about half an hour.

6. Make small popper balls out of this dough and arrange in the Air fryer basket.

7. Cook for about 15 minutes and dish out to serve warm.

Nutrition:

Calories: 385, Fat: 32.8g, Carbohydrates: 5.2g, Sugar: 0.4g, Protein: 17g, Sodium: 1532mg

Cream and Coconut Cups

Preparation Time: 15 minutes

Servings: 6

Ingredients:

- 8 oz. cream cheese, soft
- 3 eggs
- 2 tbsp. butter; melted
- 3 tbsp. coconut, shredded and unsweetened
- 4 tbsp. swerve

Directions:

1. Take a bowl and mix all the ingredients and whisk really well.
2. Divide into small ramekins, put them in the fryer and cook at 320°F and bake for 10 minutes. Serve cold

Nutrition:

Calories: 164; Fat: 4g; Fiber: 2g; Carbs: 5g; Protein: 5g

Double Layer Lemon Bars

Preparation Time: 10 minutes

Cooking Time: 25 minutes

Servings: 6

Ingredients:

For the crust:

- 1 cup coconut flour, sifted
- 1 tablespoon butter, melted

For the lemon topping:

- 3 eggs
- 2 teaspoons coconut flour, sifted

For the crust:

- ½ cup coconut oil, melted
- A pinch of salt
- Swerve, to taste

For the lemon topping:

- Swerve, to taste
- 2 teaspoons lemon zest
- ½ cup fresh lemon juice

Directions:

1. Preheat the Air fryer to 350 degree F and grease a 6-inch baking pan lightly.

2. Mix butter, swerve, salt, and oil in a bowl until foamy.

3. Stir in the coconut flour and mix until a smooth dough is formed.

4. Place the dough into the baking pan and press it thoroughly.

5. Transfer into the Air fryer and cook for about 8 minutes.

6. Meanwhile, whisk eggs with swerve, lemon zest, coconut flour and lemon juice in a bowl and mix well until smooth.

7. Pour this filling into the air fried crust and place into the Air fryer.

8. Set the Air fryer to 370 degree F and cook for about 23 minutes.

9. Cut into slices and serve.

Nutrition:

Calories: 301, Fat: 12.2g, Carbohydrates: 2.5g, Sugar: 1.4g, Protein: 8.8g, Sodium: 276mg

Lemon Cake

Preparation Time: 22 minutes

Servings: 6

Ingredients:

- 3 oz. brown sugar
- 3 oz. flour
- 1 tsp. dark chocolate; grated
- 3½ oz. butter; melted
- 3 eggs
- 1/2 tsp. lemon juice

Directions:

1. Mix all of the ingredients in a bowl.
2. Pour the mixture into a greased cake pan and place in the fryer
3. Cook at 360°F for 17 minutes. Let cake cool before serving

Ginger Cookies

Preparation Time: 10 minutes

Cooking time: 15 minutes

Servings: 12

Ingredients:

- 2 cups almond flour
- 1 cup swerve

- ¼ cup butter, melted
- 1 egg
- 2 teaspoons ginger, grated
- 1 teaspoon vanilla extract
- ¼ teaspoon nutmeg, ground
- ¼ teaspoon cinnamon powder

Directions:

1. In a bowl, mix all the Ingredients: and whisk well.
2. Spoon small balls out of this mix on a lined baking sheet that fits the air fryer lined with parchment paper and flatten them.
3. Put the sheet in the fryer and cook at 360 degrees F for 15 minutes.
4. Cool the cookies down and serve.

Nutrition:

Calories 220, fat 13, fiber 2, carbs 4, protein 3

Amaretto Cream

Preparation Time: 18 minutes

Servings: 8

Ingredients:

- 12 oz. chocolate chips
- 1 cup heavy cream
- 1 cup sugar
- 1/2 cup butter; melted

- 2 tbsp. amaretto liqueur

Directions:

1. Place all of the ingredients in a bowl and stir

2. Pour the mixture into small ramekins and place in the air fryer

3. Cook at 320°F for 12 minutes. Refrigerate / freeze for a while... best when served really cold.

Coco Mug Cake

Preparation Time: 30 minutes

Servings: 1

Ingredients:

- 1 large egg.

- 2 tbsp. granular erythritol.

- 2 tbsp. coconut flour.
- 2 tbsp. heavy whipping cream.
- ¼ tsp. baking powder.
- ¼ tsp. vanilla extract.

Directions:

1. In a 4-inch ramekin, whisk egg, then add remaining ingredients. Stir until smooth. Place into the air fryer basket.
2. Adjust the temperature to 300 Degrees F and set the timer for 25 minutes.
3. When done a toothpick should come out clean. Enjoy right out of the ramekin with a spoon. Serve warm.

Nutrition:

Calories: 237; Protein: 9.9g; Fiber: 5.0g; Fat: 16.4g; Carbs: 40.7g

Cinnamon Sugar Roasted Chickpeas

Preparation Time: 5 minutes

Cooking Time: 10 minutes

Servings: 2

Ingredients:

- 1 tbsp. sweetener
- 1 tbsp. cinnamon
- 1 C. chickpeas

Directions:

1. Preheat air fryer oven to 390 degrees.

2. Rinse and drain chickpeas.

3. Mix all ingredients together and add to air fryer.

4. Pour into the Oven rack/basket. Place the Rack on the middle-shelf of the Air fryer oven. Set temperature to 390°F, and set time to 10 minutes.

Nutrition:

Calories – 111, Protein – 16 g., Fat – 19 g., Carbs – 18 g.

Notes

CPSIA information can be obtained
at www.ICGtesting.com
Printed in the USA
BVHW090736150521
607370BV00012B/2001

9 781801 931441